GW01182477

Original title:
The Joy of Giving

Author: Ophelia Ravenscroft
ISBN HARDBACK: 978-9916-94-038-9
ISBN PAPERBACK: 978-9916-94-039-6

A Hand to Hold

A sandwich shared is twice the fun,
With every bite, our giggles run.
My friends all say, it’s a delight,
Especially when it's just a bite!

A joke, a wink, or silly dance,
This laughter grows, it takes a chance.
In every gift, there's joy so bright,
Who knew sharing could feel so light?

Light in a Handful

A cookie here, a muffin there,
My friends all know I have to share.
But when I found my stash of pie,
Selfishness whispered, “Oh, just try!”

Yet as I paused and thought it through,
I recognized the fun it grew.
For every slice I gave away,
My laughter bounced right back to play!

The Warmth We Bestow

A hat I found, with fleece so warm,
To give away it took some charm.
But once I saw my buddy freeze,
I tossed it over with such ease!

His grin was vast, his cheeks turned red,
"Are you sure?" my hat I said.
And as he wore it, laughter flew,
That warmth was doubled, who knew?

Seeds of Selflessness

I planted seeds with hope galore,
To see who'd share my garden floor.
With every sprout, a smile would bloom,
You take one too, for more room!

As veggies grew, my friends would cheer,
With zucchini and squash held dear.
But often they’d ask for something sweet,
A pie to share, that can't be beat!

Radiant Acts

A llama in a tutu danced one day,
He gifted cupcakes, hip-hip-hooray!
The sprinkles flew, oh what a sight,
His friends all laughed, pure delight.

A parrot sang in silly rhyme,
Gave out hugs, it's party time!
With twirls and spins, they pranced around,
In this crazy joy, love abounds.

The Heart's Embrace

A cat in glasses read a book,
Gave wisdom out, that silly look!
He purred and shared his favorite tale,
Of fishy dreams, no need to sail.

A dog with socks upon his paws,
Shared squeaky toys without a pause.
They tossed and tumbled, laughed galore,
In this wild fun, who could ask for more?

Flames of Generosity

A squirrel with nuts, oh what a sight,
Shared them freely, day and night.
The chipmunks cheered, their cheeks were stuffed,
In this nutty tale, hearts were puffed.

A raccoon found a shiny spoon,
Gave it to a bird, who sang a tune.
With a wink and a smile, the party spread,
In these strange joys, all worries fled.

A Symphony of Giving

A frog in a top hat croaked a beat,
He offered flies as a tasty treat.
The band of bugs began to play,
In this melody, fun led the way.

A turtle lent his shell to paint,
Transformed his friends, a silly saint.
With colors bright and laughter high,
In this joyful art, spirits fly.

A Reflection of Love

A quirky cat wore a bow,
Gifting mice, as you know.
Dance and prance, not a care,
Yet the mice still scream in scare.

With every treat, a snarky wink,
Puppy pals wait by the sink.
Cake for you, and crumbs for me,
Who knew sharing could be so free?

Champagne flows from a soda can,
I toast to life and that’s the plan.
Balloons rise, and laughter too,
Just don’t let them pop on you!

So here’s to fun in what we do,
Sharing silliness, it’s true.
In every giggle, every hug,
Is love wrapped up—you get the bug!

The Harmony of Generosity

A parrot dressed in a hat,
Gifts a cracker to the cat.
They share a drink of lemonade,
While the sun begins to fade.

A silly clown on a tricycle,
Spreads candy that's oh-so-psychical.
His wig a rainbow, bright and bold,
Sharing giggles in the cold.

An octopus shares a big red sock,
With each tentacle, he takes stock.
'This is mine!' a fishy cries,
Yet all share in this messy prize.

With every laugh, a gift we bring,
Softly hum the song of spring.
In chuckles, quirks, and silly strife,
We find the best gifts in our life!

The Canvas of Connection

A toddler scribbles with delight,
Colors spill into the light.
She gives a painting to a frog,
Who hops around just like a dog.

Two squirrels plan a nutty feast,
They argue over which is least.
Then share their stash with all in tow,
In chaos, friendship starts to grow.

A zebra dreams in polka dots,
And shares her style with all the tots.
With rainbow stripes, they dance and spin,
In every twirl lies joy within.

So paint the world in hues so bright,
With quirky friendships, pure delight.
For giving laughs, and smiles too,
Are treasures worth much more than blue!

An Inklings of Kindness

A penguin with a big red bow,
Waddles fast, just to show.
He slips on ice, falls with flair,
Gifts a fish with a comedic air.

A bear wears shades, thinks he’s cool,
But when he tumbles, it’s far from rule.
A basket full of honey lands,
Shared with friends—a sweet demand!

Bunnies bake a cake so bright,
Yet it ends up in a playful fight.
Flour flies, and frosting spreads,
Laughing all the way to beds.

So as we play and pile on fun,
Sharing joy, we're never done.
In every wink and playful jive,
Together, we truly come alive!

The Generous Spirit

With cookies baked and gifts galore,
I knocked on doors, delight to score.
But when they saw my cheer-filled face,
They quickly hid, a quiet chase.

I left a note on a few roofs,
'If you’re out, I’ll take your pooches!'
But I just wanted to lend a hand,
Not turn their dogs to my own band!

Each time I share my quirky snacks,
My neighbors run, and that’s a fact!
Yet hearts are warm, they know my name,
My fondness for pranks, my silly game.

So here’s to fun in all we do,
A sprinkle of joy, a laugh or two.
For kindness wrapped in humor bold,
Is the best gift that one can hold.

Soulful Giveaways

I brought my friend some fancy socks,
They sported monkeys doing knocks.
He laughed so hard, he nearly cried,
'Only you, my friend, could provide!'

In turn, he gifted me a hat,
That looked just like a giant cat.
We strolled around, a silly sight,
Two pals in fashion, full of light.

With homemade jams, we tried to share,
But soon the squirrels began to stare.
They swarmed us fast, a fluffy horde,
And left us with just one small hoard.

So here’s our vow, we giggled loud,
To share with hearts but not our crowd.
For joy is found in each wild thing,
When laughter comes from every fling.

Kinship of Hearts

I gifted my neighbor a plant so green,
He thanked me like I ruled the scene.
But when it wilted, oh what a fuss,
He swore ‘til death it was a bust!

Then came the day he brought me stew,
It looked like mud, but was it true?
He chuckled loud as he set it down,
'Nothing says love like brown in town!'

We swapped our dishes and had a blast,
Each meal an adventure, unsurpassed.
With flavors funny, and textures odd,
We'd toast each other, cheering God!

In this kinship of quirky delights,
We found our fun on chilly nights.
For love is laughter, and silly games,
Strange concoctions, but no one blames!

Moments of Unselfishness

I offered my friend a slice of cake,
He grinned and said, 'Oh for goodness' sake!'
It wobbled a bit, like jelly and jam,
'You made this?' he asked, 'You're quite the ham!'

In return, he gave me a shirt with spots,
That clashed with everything, even pots!
We wore them proudly, like true best mates,
Dancing in public, despite all fates.

Each act of kindness, a joke in disguise,
We'd wave to folks with googly eyes.
Laughter sparked like bright summer days,
Turned our clumsy ways into a craze.

So let's toast to the silly and sweet,
To moments we share, a kindred beat.
For in the humor of our daily grind,
The true gift of life's the laughter we find.

Threads of Joy

In a world of mismatched socks,
I gift you the ones with silly clocks.
A laugh erupts, oh what a sight,
Two crazed pairs, and we both take flight.

With cookies shaped like a cat's meow,
I share them all, I take a bow.
You munch and grunt, it's quite a sight,
Your crumbs and giggles, pure delight.

A book of puns, a treasure chest,
I share the worst, I do my best.
You groan and chuckle, laughter spills,
These moments shared, my heart it heals.

So swap those quirks, don't be shy,
A friendship rich, oh me, oh my!
With threads of joy, our hearts entwine,
In this funny dance, forever shine.

The Abundance of Sharing

A pie split thrice, a sight to see,
I took the crust, and you took the glee.
We both held spoons, a sugary fight,
Together we laughed, oh what a bite!

With candy bars, I dare to share,
But not the nuts—those I can't bear!
You roll your eyes, a playful frown,
Yet munching on almonds, you wear a crown.

Let’s swap our snacks, a glorious mess,
I'll take the chips, you wear the stress.
Crunching and munching, giggles ensue,
In this silly game, we both win too!

So raise a toast with fizzy pop,
A bubbly day, we’ll never stop.
With each shared bite, our laughter grows,
In this joy of jest, true friendship flows.

A Canvas of Compassion

A canvas bright, with paint so bold,
I gift you swirls, a sight to behold.
You splash blue here, red goes there,
Creating chaos, with flair to spare.

My brushes dance, your laughter rings,
We paint our dreams, on colorful wings.
A masterpiece born, of giggles and cheer,
In silly splashes, our bond draws near.

With brushes lost in a splendid mess,
You painted my nose, I must confess.
We laugh till we cry, and smear some more,
Art’s not so serious, it’s never a chore.

So let’s mix colors, and toss the fears,
We’ll paint a world, that lasts for years.
In every stroke, love’s laughter gleams,
The canvas of life, filled with dreams.

Bridges of Goodwill

With spaghetti strands, we share a bite,
Two slurpers here, a glorious sight.
Noodles like bridges, twist and twine,
As we laugh and noodle, we draw a line.

A wink and a nudge, with a friendly tease,
I gift you my peas, a plate full of freeze.
You grimace and chuckle, a playful shock,
But together we feast, around the clock.

Our friendship's a buffet, an endless spread,
With each little quirk, our laughter's fed.
So let's build a bridge made of funny delights,
Connecting our hearts on these joyous nights.

From silly dinners to sips at dawn,
We gather our moments, fondly drawn.
In every bite, goodwill ignites,
Together we bloom, in pure delight.

Kind Acts in Quiet Places

In a corner of the park, a sandwich was shared,
A pigeon looked shocked, acted quite unprepared.
A child tossed some crumbs, with giggles galore,
While squirrels around danced, asking for more.

A lady lost her hat, right under a tree,
A dog picked it up, as proud as can be.
With a wag of his tail, he returned it in style,
The crowd burst in laughter, oh, what a while!

A Tapestry of Giving

A grandma knits socks for the gnomes in her yard,
Who wear them in spring, looking oh-so-retard.
Each stitch tells a joke, with a wink in the thread,
As they prance in delight, upon small mushroom beds.

A cat steals a pickle from under the table,
The dog, on a mission, starts chasing the fable.
Neighbor joins the fray, tossing peas from his plate,
Now there’s a veggie parade, isn’t that great?

Embracing Abundance

A baker made cupcakes, but forgot all the sugar,
He offered them free, like a wholesome intruder.
Folks lined up in droves, for a taste of the shade,
With sprinkles of giggles, a strange pastry trade.

A juggler tossed apples, while riding a bike,
Hit a tree, lost a balance, oh boy, what a strike!
With laughter erupting, and joy in the air,
They shared bits of fruit, without any care.

Colors of Connection

Two friends with paint, decided to splatter,
Ended up colorful, in a funny matter.
With splashes of red, and a twist of some blue,
They painted the dog, who now felt brand new.

A gardener with seeds, thought she'd sow a big laugh,
Grew flowers that sang, with a silly giraffe.
Neighbors came to peek, at the site of a show,
A garden of giggles, oh where will it go?

Hidden Treasures of Compassion

In a world of toys and treasures,
A cookie jar with hidden pleasures.
I gave my friend a slice of pie,
And watched their eyes grow wide and spry.

With each small gift, my heart grows light,
Like tinfoil hats that shine so bright.
The laughter shared, a priceless gain,
As hugs are tossed like candy rain.

Pasta tossed in silly shapes,
A fruit bouquet of goofy grapes.
They said that kindness costs a dime,
But I just call it playful time.

So share a snack or dance a jig,
A silly hat, or dress a pig.
For every giggle that we send,
We find the treasures that won't end.

Ripples of Generosity

A rubber ducky on the lake,
Floats on, giggling, for fun’s sake.
I tossed a coin with perfect aim,
And watched it splash like silly fame.

With every gift, a splash anew,
Like water we churn in a shoe.
A wink, a grin, my friend will cheer,
They thought the joke would disappear!

To donate socks, a fashion craze,
With stripes and polka dots—a blaze!
The world’s a stage, a quirky scene,
Where kindness reigns, bright and serene.

And if you slip on a banana peel,
It’s not the fall, but how you feel.
We spread the vibes; let laughter flow,
In this great dance of give and glow.

Sunshine for the Soul

A sunflower dance and pots of stew,
I made a feast for folks like you.
With pies that jiggle, cakes that twist,
Who knew that kindness had such a twist?

A squirt of whipped cream on my chin,
I serve up giggles, let the fun begin!
Look at me now, I'm chef supreme,
With laughter layered like a dream.

A sprinkle here, a pinch of cheer,
The neighbors stop by with a hearty jeer.
They bring their cats, a furry crew,
And suddenly, it's a kindness zoo!

So come on over, bring your smile,
We'll dance and laugh for a while.
For in the fun, our hearts take flight,
Spreading warmth and pure delight.

Moments of Warmth

In a park where puppies play,
I tossed my worries far away.
I shared my snack, a crumb or two,
And watched a squirrel join the crew.

A knitted hat with silly ears,
Is worth a thousand silly cheers.
When friends all gather, it's never bland,
For every hug is carefully planned.

A pie-filled face is quite the sight,
As laughter lifts us, pure delight.
When smiles abound, our hearts ignite,
We dance through life, all day and night.

So share a moment, take a seat,
With every giggle, life's so sweet.
A touch of warmth is all we need,
To make the world a kinder breed.

Hearts in Harmony

In a land where socks would dance,
I found some shoes that dream of prance.
I wrapped them up in shiny foil,
And sent them off with a big ol' coil.

A cat with boots and a fish in a hat,
They laughed and played, imagine that!
The joy of sharing makes them sing,
Oh, what a crazy, funny thing!

A grandma’s cookies, a runaway pie,
I tossed them gently, oh my, oh my!
They landed flat on Uncle Joe,
But his smile grew; oh what a show!

So if you find a toy or two,
Just wrap it up and send to who?
Laughter echoes through the room,
In this wild sharing, there’s no gloom!

A Feather's Touch

With a feather gently tickling noses,
I wrapped up joy in a box of roses.
I passed it round, it made folks squeal,
A hiccup of laughter was the deal!

I found a sock that danced and spun,
And sent it to my neighbor's son.
He wore it proudly on his head,
And off he went, filled with dread!

A rubber duck in a bubble bath,
Found its way to a jolly path.
It quacked a tune, oh what a show,
As kids joined in, don’t you know!

So sprinkle laughter like confetti bright,
With every gift, you'll spark delight.
In this wacky world of smiles and clucks,
It’s truly fun to share the ducks!

When We Share

A pie that flew across the night,
Gained wings and vanished, oh what a sight!
We laughed and gasped, where could it be?
The joy of sharing is plain to see!

A bunch of grapes all wore their hats,
They rolled and tumbled like acrobats.
In the kitchen, giggles would flare,
Each piece of fruit showed they could care.

A treasure chest filled with silly socks,
We tossed them in, what laughter knocks!
The more we tossed, the more we cheered,
In this parade of fun, we're all endeared!

So let’s embrace this playful spirit,
Sharing merriment, you’ll want to hear it.
With secrets wrapped in funny wraps,
We'll start a joy that never maps!

Kindred Spirits

In a world where jellybeans bloom,
I shared my stash, banished the gloom.
The sugar rush made everyone swoon,
As we floated high like a cartoon!

A dancing broom joined our little choir,
With every step, we climbed higher.
We twirled and laughed till we fell,
Sharing whimsy, oh so swell!

A pizza party with silly hats,
Sparklers on cake, oh imagine that!
We swapped our slices, oh what fun,
In each bite, laughter had begun!

So if you seek a spark of glee,
Just grab your friends and share with me.
In this quirky rhythm, we all place bets,
On the fun we've shared, with no regrets!

The Warm Glow Within

A penny here, a nickel there,
You'd think I'm made of fresh hot air!
I tossed a dime to help a cat,
She looked at me and said, "What's that?"

With cupcakes piled and gifts in tow,
I planned a party, but there's no dough!
I gave my friend a noodle hug,
She cooked it up; it turned outugly.

A high-five sent across the room,
Left everyone to share the gloom.
But laughter bubbled, joy did flow,
That's worth much more than cash, you know!

So here's to fun in every deed,
Like planting smiles, we plant a seed.
With silly hats and socks to share,
We find our riches—beyond compare!

A Tidal Wave of Kindness

I spilled my coffee—what a sight!
Yet the barista said, "That's all right!"
He handed me a straw and grin,
"Just sip and swim; let the fun begin!"

On the beach, I tossed a ball,
But misfired—what a clumsy fall!
A seagull caught it, took it away,
I chased him down, shouting, "Hey!"

A splash of joy among the waves,
Each drop a blessing, as it saves.
We built a castle, oh so grand,
With moats of laughter and our band.

So ride the tides of giving bright,
With ocean waves, let's share delight.
Embrace the mess, make it a blast,
In kindness' wave, we're never last!

Reverberations of Hope

With a rubber chicken in my bag,
I went to cheer, but got a wag.
A whistle here, a kazoo there,
What's that sound? Oh, don't you dare!

A tap dance that went all astray,
As I tried to give my heart away.
I stumbled, fell, bounced back like gum,
Laughter echoed; oh, what fun!

A jingle-jangle, jolly spree,
With dances made for you and me.
No big speeches, just silly glee,
In every chuckle, we set hearts free.

So let us sing and make some noise,
Share the love with all our joys.
In foolish acts, the hope will rise,
With goofy grins and twinkling eyes!

Comets of Charity

In the sky, a comet flashes,
I thought of gifts, but time just crashes!
I tossed a toy that landed neat,
Right on a dog—what a treat!

A kindness rocket, zooming wide,
I launched it high, it took a ride.
Down in the park, it burst with cheer,
But left the pigeons—quaking in fear!

With silly strings all tied in knots,
We marched along, sharing our thoughts.
A giggle here, a dance so bright,
We turned the day into pure delight.

So let's be comets, wild and free,
Spread our warmth like a bumblebee.
In giving spree, let's have some fun,
In laughter's wake, we'll be the one!

Tapestry of Giving

A sock for a mug, what a strange gift,
Wrapped up in paper, it gives quite a lift!
My cat got a collar, it glittered and shone,
Now he struts with swagger like he's on loan!

Pancakes for lunch, why not, I decree!
With sprinkles and syrup, a syrupy spree!
Grandma thought it genius to bake with her care,
But I left with a cat who was stuck in a chair!

Each gag gift we share, here's a new twist,
Like a rubber chicken when morning's dismissed.
Laughter ignites when we trip on our toes,
In the wacky world where love freely flows!

So bring forth the laughter and strange little charms,
For hilarity lives where affection warms.
In a tapestry woven of giggles and cheer,
We dance in delight every day of the year!

Nourished by Compassion

I brought you a stew but dropped it outside,
Now it's more of a splatter, that's my chef's pride!
A plant for your desk, nice and leafy, so bright,
Turns out it’s a cactus, a prickly fright!

My friend loves to bake, donate cookies they say,
But they always forget to whisk, oh dear, what a day!
When cookies become cobwebs, and crumbles galore,
We feast on the giggles, what else is in store?

A gift from the heart that didn’t quite stick,
Like glitter on sweaters, now that’s a neat trick!
To share silly moments while kindness will bloom,
With comrades beside, there’s no room for gloom!

So here’s to the oops and the parts that go wrong,
With laughter our bond, how we all belong!
In the chaos of sharing, a belly will ache,
For compassion’s pure humor is what we all make!

The Ripple of Kindness

Dropped my sandwich; it flew like a kite,
Right into the lunch where a squirrel took flight!
With crumbs on my shirt and a grin way too wide,
I'll share my mishaps; come join in the ride!

A funny old hat with a feather so bright,
I gifted it boldly, it's quite a sight!
Now all of our friends have gathered around,
They're wondering loudly if I can be found!

We tossed candy canes in a pool full of goo,
Wishing that every splash brings sweet joy anew.
With each wave of laughter the ripples go wide,
Unity grows when we all join the ride!

With kindness aflutter and smiles all around,
Compassion's the treasure we've all come to found.
In moments so quirky, in silliness shared,
We'll spread love and giggles, feeling light and bared!

Cherished Moments

A mismatched pair of socks, it warmed my cold feet,
And stickers from strangers, is life so sweet!
With crayons and laughter, we colored the sky,
Check out our rainbow, or don't, we won't cry!

My grandma said "You make a mean potpourri,"
But it turned out to smell like old shoes, oh me!
When gifts are not perfect, we laugh and we cheer,
A hug and a smile are what really brings near!

A day at the park, with balloons going high,
While I chased them down as they drifted on by.
In moments like these, we choose to embrace,
The funny experiences that time can't erase!

So let's find our quirkiness, love strong and true,
As cherished connections bring magic anew.
For in the silly times and laughter deep-seated,
Are memories shared, never to be defeated!

Embracing Empathy

In a land of mismatched socks,
Laughter spills like a pot of rocks.
Sharing snacks and silly hats,
We toast to joy with fuzzy cats.

With every giggle, hearts grow wide,
Like balloons that go for a ride.
A pinch of kindness, a dash of cheer,
Makes every frown disappear.

From lending crayons to petting pups,
We fill the world with cheerful cups.
As we trip over friendly toes,
The warmth of caring brightly glows.

So here's to laughter, wild and free,
Sprinkling joy like confetti!
In this circus of life, we play,
With smiles and kindness every day.

A Dance with Generosity

In the kitchen, pots collide,
Flour flies like a butterfly ride.
Cookies baking, oh what fun,
The dance of giving has begun!

With silly moves and cupcake spins,
Everyone wins when we share wins.
Joey trips but finds a cake,
And all our hearts begin to break!

A sprinkle here, a dash of that,
Our plates piled high, ‘til they splat!
Laughter echoes as we play,
All hearts sound like they’re on display.

Dancing through the joyful mess,
We’ll give our all, nothing less!
A pinch of laughter, a scoop of grace,
Fill the room with a warm embrace.

Fill the World with Love

With a waddle and a flap, we strut,
Hand in hand and not a single rut.
We spread the cheer with jellybeans,
In our quirky, colorful scenes.

From tiny gifts to grand bouquets,
Laughter bubbles in weirdest ways.
Frogs in hats and ducks in suits,
Generosity that truly roots!

When hearts are light, we dance around,
With silly songs, joy can be found.
So let's shout out from the hills,
Together in laughter, our hearts it fills.

Spread the love like jam on toast,
With every giggle, we'll raise a toast!
In the zoo of life, we are the vine,
Twining together, oh how we shine!

Unseen Threads of Grace

In a shoe shop where all shoes squeak,
We share the giggles and the cheek.
With mismatched laces, oh what a sight,
We stumble forth, our souls alight.

Like a clown car packed with cheer,
Rolling on, we've naught to fear.
A kind word thrown, a wink or a nod,
A ripple of goodwill, oh my God!

Through the maze of silly dreams,
We hold together like sticky creams.
In laughter's arms, we find our pace,
With unseen threads, we interlace.

So let's be silly, let's be bold,
In this tapestry of hearts, pure gold.
With every gesture, small or grand,
We weave a world, hand in hand.

A Circle of Smiles

I found an old sock, all tattered and worn,
I wrapped it in ribbons, a gift for my corn.
The corn looked confused, like it got quite the fright,
But hey, it felt special, and that seemed just right.

I baked a big pie, just to share with the flies,
They danced in a frenzy, excitement in their eyes.
But when I took a bite, they flew off in dismay,
Guess my giving skills need a little more play!

A rock in my pocket, I thought it might charm,
So I gave it a name, and I hoped it'd bring calm.
When I tossed it to Fred, he sighed with delight,
But it landed on Tim, now that's not quite right!

In the garden, I gifted a sprout saying "grow,"
It chuckled and wiggled, then put on a show.
A tangle of laughter, a riot of glee,
Who knew being generous could be such a spree!

The Art of Altruism

I found a big box of old candy canes,
I wrapped them in sparkles, tied up with some chains.
I offered one to Lou, who passed one to Sue,
But the peppermint army declared war on the crew!

I gifted my cat a plush mouse in disguise,
She gave me a look, like "Really? Surprise?"
But then she took off, with a leap and a flip,
Translating my kindness to a wild kitty trip!

I shared my leftover cake, it was a delight,
But the squirrels thought it was their party tonight.
They took all the frosting, left crumbs on the floor,
Now my cake has a tale, and I'm left wanting more!

With joy in my heart, I gave my best broom,
It danced 'round the house, swept away all my gloom.
But it took off in a hurry, chasing leaves like a fool,
Now I'm here with a mop, that's the magic of drool!

Whispers of Benevolence

I painted some rocks, all colorful, bright,
Left them in the park, felt like pure delight.
Then a kid took a peek, thought they were a snack,
Now there's one rock less, oh, that's kind of slack!

On a rainy cool day, I thought, let's have fun,
I gifted my neighbor a bright plastic bun.
She laughed so loud, said "Is this a real treat?"
I said, "Only if you add a dash of defeat!"

A bottle of bubbles, I shared with a bear,
He popped every one, didn't seem to care.
Then he sneezed with dismay, which scattered the fun,
Now we have a bubble-less bear on the run!

I gave my old socks to a tree, with a grin,
The tree looked quite puzzled, where do I begin?
But with every breeze, it swayed with pure joy,
Now it's the trendiest tree, oh boy, oh boy!

Lanterns of Light

I made little lanterns, all crafted with care,
I handed them out, to folks unaware.
But when one caught fire, it lit up the night,
Now we've got bonfires and a party in sight!

A basket of laughter, I took to the zoo,
The monkeys grabbed it all, they knew what to do.
They flung it like frisbees, oh, what a great show,
Now the giraffes giggle, watching chaos below.

I gave my old sweater to a cold little frog,
He waddled around in it, feeling like a blog.
He croaked out a tune, went viral for days,
Now he's the fashion icon, in amphibian ways!

With joy in my heart, I shared silly caps,
The dogs wore them proudly, making some slaps.
They pranced through the park, with style so divine,
Who knew giving laughter didn't cost a dime!

The Art of Sharing

A sandwich split, a soda too,
A friend says, "Hey, I want some too!"
We laugh and munch, but oh surprise,
Now there’s crumbs in all our fries!

I gift you laughter, you gift me cheer,
Together we create our giggles here.
A wink, a smile, we trade like cards,
Even if you steal my candy bars!

With every swap, our jokes do grow,
Like silly hats we wear in tow.
Let’s share a joke or two or three,
Until we’re laughing like crazy bees!

So here’s to us, the sharing crew,
With goofy antics always in view.
Who knew that giving could be this fun?
Let's spread the joy, we’ve only just begun!

Blossoms of Benevolence

A cupcake tossed and icing flies,
Landing right on someone's eyes!
"Surprise!" I laugh, you laugh back loud,
A sweet delight, we're sugar proud!

We share our treats, with sticky hands,
Trading bites like silly bands.
A sprinkle here, a frosting there,
Our laughter echoes in the air!

You brought the joy, I took your fries,
Together we make the best of pies.
With funny faces and silly tunes,
We dance like flowers under balloons!

So here's to blossoms that freely bloom,
In every heart, there's always room.
Let's share our sweets and make a scene,
Bringing laughter, you and me, a team!

Overflowing Baskets

A basket full, what a sight to see,
Filled with goods for you and me.
We grab a snack, we don't think twice,
Sharing popcorn, oh, isn't that nice?

Bananas fly and apples roll,
"Catch that orange!" is our goal.
We giggle as we run around,
In this circus, joy is found!

With every bite, we swap a grin,
Like a game we're dying to win.
A fruit fight here, a laugh attack,
Watch out for the grape, it's coming back!

So stack our treats in a colorful heap,
There's plenty to share, and none to keep.
In this fruity world, let's make a scene,
With laughter shared, we're a happy team!

Harmony in Giving

With every hug, we give and cheer,
Heartbeat smiles as we draw near.
A boisterous shout as gifts we toss,
“Don’t drop it now, or we’re both lost!”

You take my scarf, I wear your cap,
What a picture of fun and flap!
With mismatched socks and silly shoes,
Giving style is how we choose!

We swap our secrets, share our dreams,
Turn each moment to funny themes.
A tickle here, a surprise there,
Joy in sharing floats in the air!

So here’s the beat of harmony,
In each exchange, we’re truly free.
With hearts so light, we dance and play,
In our bright world, joy leads the way!

Fountains of Kindness

In a town where smiles are free,
People toss joy like confetti.
Balloons floated high in the sky,
As laughter bounced by—oh my!

A dog found a shoe, then danced with glee,
Chasing children, wild and free.
Old Joe baked cookies, one for all,
And tripped on his cat—what a fall!

The fountain bubbled, spritzing cheer,
While neighbors shared snacks, loud and clear.
All gathered round for a cheerful feast,
'Til the squirrel nabbed the last piece of yeast!

With every hug, a funny twist,
The more we share, the more we missed.
Like socks that vanish in the dryer,
The joy we share just keeps getting higher!

Embraced by Generosity

Benny the bee stole honey for fun,
Leaving his hive, he thought he’d outrun.
But sweet sticky stuff dripped in his wake,
While flowers laughed at the mess he'd make!

Grace baked a pie, it smelled divine,
To share the treats she felt quite fine.
But out jumped a cat with a salty glare,
And hid the dessert—oh, the despair!

At the park, each swing had a buddy,
Sliding down made their tummies all muddy.
The swing set broke—what a sight to behold,
As the kids cheered, laughing loud and bold!

With every blooper and silly slip,
They found pure joy in each funny trip.
Generosity danced along the way,
Creating memories that forever stay!

A Heart Unwrapped

With paper ripped and ribbons all askew,
Billy thought of pranks he could do.
A bat as a gift, quite fittingly strange,
His friend giggled loud, “Now that’s a change!”

A sock puppet show, the act of the year,
Both friends in stitches, it’s quite clear.
They wrapped up their laughter like treasures unfurled,
Turning dull moments into a wild whirl!

At Grandma's day, they brought her a cake,
But the frosting was gone—oh what a mistake!
With sprinkles and smiles, they danced all around,
While Grandma’s old cat chased the crumbs on the ground!

So open your heart, share laughter and care,
Wrapped in kindness, spread joy everywhere.
Each silly moment adds to the heap,
Creating a memory that’s yours to keep!

Gifts of Kindness

The postman slipped on a banana peel,
But instead of anger, we all chose to squeal.
Packages flying, confusion ensued,
A gift of laughter, we all felt renewed!

Tom brought donuts with a sparkle or two,
But they vanished quick, as donuts will do.
The cat on the counter gave a sly peek,
As crumbs turned to treasures for all with a tweak!

At the party, a hat that was lost,
Reappeared on a dog—oh what a cost!
With laughter and cheers, they took it in stride,
As joy wrapped around like a fun, crazy ride!

In every mishap, a kindness might float,
Like balloons in the breeze, they dance and they gloat.
So pack up your giggles, give them away,
For gifts of delight make the world brighter each day!

Gifts of Heart

When I found a sock beneath my bed,
I wrapped it up, just like I said.
I gave it to a friend for fun,
Now he wears it on the run.

A half-eaten cake, I called it art,
With sprinkles on top, it's a sweet start.
They laughed so hard, they almost cried,
Who knew leftovers could be so wide!

A pencil with a wobbly lead,
I thought it suits my friend's bright head.
He drew a mustache on his cat,
Now that's a gift—I'll take a spat!

The little things that come from me,
Make people smile, oh can't you see?
From funny trinkets to silly fads,
I spread the cheer, so none feels bad.

Threads of Generosity

I knitted a sweater that’s two sizes wide,
A rainbow explosion, I took in my stride.
When my friend wore it, oh what a sight!
A fashion disaster that gave pure delight!

I painted a mug with a llama's face,
Took it to work, oh what a disgrace!
My colleagues laughed till the coffee spilt,
That’s one more reason for my mug to wilt!

I wrapped up some rocks with a bow on top,
I said, "These are gems!" I just couldn’t stop.
When they unwrapped, they gave me a glare,
But trust me, folks, I just had to share!

A bow tie made out of pasta and cheese,
I wore it proudly! Their laughter won't cease.
So here's to gifts that are silly and bright,
They lighten the day, and that's pure delight!

Echoes of Kindness

I found a parrot, quite full of sass,
I thought, 'What a gift!' as I watched him pass.
He squawked my secrets and stories from school,
Now I’m the butt of every bird's duel!

A dance lesson gift, I did not expect,
But two left feet, what a weird effect!
My partner fell down, we rolled on the floor,
We laughed so hard, we could not take more!

A surprise bouquet of wilted greens,
With gummy worms and a few magazines.
They smiled and asked if it’s all I brought,
“Just wait until you see the next thought!”

I offered my crayons; they’re all broken, true!
But each funky color can spark something new.
So here’s to the echoes of laughter and cheer,
When gifts are a giggle, you hold them so dear!

A Handful of Smiles

I gathered some smiles in a little jar,
When I opened it up, they traveled afar.
Floating like bubbles, they scattered around,
A giggle explosion, there's joy to be found!

A pair of socks with holes galore,
I claimed they're vintage; who could want more?
Wrapped them in paper, gave them away,
Now they own fashion—who needs to be gray?

A jar of pickles, I thought, 'What the heck!'
This "treat" I brought surely raised a few necks.
They dared me to try, I took a big bite,
Now pickles define our hilarious night!

So gifts come in forms that often surprise,
Like kindness and laughter, oh they're the prize.
When a handful of smiles is all that you need,
Share fun with the world—just spread the good deed!

Lanterns in the Dark

In the attic I found an old hat,
Pour in the snacks, now that's a fat cat!
Toss a few cookies, watch him delight,
As shadows dance wildly, oh what a sight!

The neighbor's dog howls at my tree,
Looks like he thinks it’s a feast for free!
With a wink and a grin, I hand him a bone,
Now we are partners, both fully grown!

Everyone’s laughing, it’s quite the scene,
Even my goldfish is feeling quite keen!
When laughter starts echoing through the night,
You know that the fun is just taking flight!

A lantern for you, one for me too,
Let’s light up the night, with giggles in view!
With joy flowing freely, like sparkling spark,
We’ll dance till the dawn, our own little lark!

Seeds of Delight

I’ve got some old shoes, they’ve seen better days,
But plant them with seeds, and watch nature play!
A garden of sneakers, as weird as can be,
With tomatoes that giggle and beans full of glee!

My buddy came over, he stared and he grinned,
He threw me a shovel, said, "Let’s see how they’ve sinned!"
We dug up the lawn, made a mess of the place,
Creating odd veggies with smiles on their face!

Lettuce with hats and peppers that dance,
We laughed ‘til we cried, it was quite a chance.
With such silly growth, our garden's a hit,
Neighbors stop by, and they can’t handle it!

Seeds of delight, in shoes and in dreams,
We share all the harvest, with giggles and screams!
A salad of joy, so puzzling and bright,
Let’s toast to the strange, and carry the light!

Whispers of Altruism

A squirrel once chattered, all puffed and proud,
Claiming his stash, he was quite the loud!
I offered him nuts, said, "Please be my mate!"
He dropped all his acorns, and danced like a plate!

With chatter and squeaks, we planned a grand feast,
Inviting the birds, but not the wild beast.
A table of twigs, covered in seeds,
We shared all the snacks, fulfilling our needs!

The sky went from blue to a shimmering gold,
While critters all gathered, the stories retold.
What's better than sharing a sweet little bite?
It brings all the laughter, as stars start to light!

Who knew a few nuts could spark up such fun?
When critters unite, hearts twirl like a bun.
They'll whisper to you, as they wiggle and sway,
In the joy of our kindness, we'll all find our way!

When Hearts Combine

Two kids with a plan on a warm sunny day,
Set off on a mission, come what may.
With cookies in hand, they knock on a door,
The sweet taste of kindness, who could ask for more?

They bartered some laughs for a cup of sweet tea,
The old man just chuckled, oh what a spree!
He shared tales of yore, while munching on treats,
Adventures and mischief, and stories so sweet!

A tip of his hat for the friendship they shared,
With crumbs on their faces, they knew that they dared.
They bounced down the street, a dance in their feet,
Leaving giggles behind, oh, what a sweet feat!

When hearts come together, like sunshine and rain,
They brighten the world, causing joy and no pain.
So let's share our cookies, our laughter and smiles,
In the stories we weave, we'll go many miles!

Dancing on Generosity

With a twirl and a swirl, I hand you a cake,
Made of cardboard and icing, oh what a mistake!
You laugh, I laugh, we both start to spin,
In the world of odd gifts, we both seem to win.

A sock puppet surprise with a googly eye,
You wear it on your hand, oh my, oh my!
We dance around joy in our mismatched shoes,
Giving out chuckles, too good to refuse.

A bag of old buttons, they jingle and jive,
You barter a dance, oh what a way to thrive!
We trade silly treasures, all odd and bizarre,
In this wacky world, our hearts will go far.

So let's keep on frolicking, sharing our cheer,
With gifts full of laughter, and a tic-tac-toe deer!
In this madcap frolic, we find some delight,
In the dance of the playful, we take off in flight.

An Offering of the Heart

I brought you a potted plant, it's plastic, you see,
With a smile on my face, I presented with glee.
You squint, and you laugh, 'It won't grow any leaves!'
But the joy of my gift, oh, that's what it weaves!

A sweater with holes, it's more air than cloth,
You wear it while laughing, not one bit sloth.
We twirl and we giggle, it fits just so right,
An offering so odd, it brings pure delight.

A jar full of buttons, some rusty, some bright,
You trade me a lemon that's oddly half-white.
We barter our quirks in this game called 'fun',
In the heart of the jest, we're never outdone.

My gift is your laughter, your giggle, your cheer,
Through strange little offerings, we draw friends near.
In this merry exchange, we've both won the game,
As the heart opens wide, it feels never the same.

Gardens of Gratitude

In my garden of treasures that sparkle and shine,
I planted a rubber chicken, one of a kind.
It clucks in the breeze, it's a glorious sight,
Who knew quirky gifts could bring so much light?

I watered my garden with old bits of laughter,
Each weed that I pulled brought more joy ever after.
You came with a joke, I replied with a grin,
In this patch of delight, we both danced right in.

Strange flowers now sprout in this beautiful mess,
With petals of giggles and roots of finesse.
We'll harvest the fun, let it bloom in the sun,
In generous gardens, we both feel like one.

So join me, dear friend, in this whimsical space,
Where the blooms of our kindness leave a funny trace.
In the fields of our hearts, where the laughter's not shy,
We plant seeds of good cheer as the crows pass us by.

The Unseen Harvest

In my basket of favors, a pickle in tow,
I offer it gleefully, you laugh, ‘Oh no!’
But with every odd gift, a giggle will spread,
As we savor the moments, more fun than the bread.

A postcard from Mars, with stamps from the moon,
You chuckle, ‘It’s out of this world, can’t come too soon!’
Each quirky exchange becomes the talk of the town,
In the unseen harvest, we share silly crowns.

A sandwich that’s made from two slices of air,
We pack it with jokes and a dash of good flair.
You take a big bite and pretend it’s a feast,
In this banquet of laughter, we both are the least.

So let’s toast with our imaginations so bright,
To gifts that are odd but bring pure delight.
For in sharing our quirks, we gather and weave,
The unseen harvest of joy that we believe.

Beneath the Giving Tree

Beneath the tree, gifts grow like weeds,
A parrot squawks, "One more, if you please!"
With bags full of goodies, we start to cheer,
Last year's fruitcake? Oh no, not that here!

A squirrel sneaks by with his eye on a snack,
While I search my pockets, what do I lack?
A hat with a joke, just to make 'em grin,
But landing on my head? It's a cat, not a win!

We trade all our treasures, from socks to old chins,
Laughter quotes from our paper-thin skins.
In funny old fashion, we giggle and sway,
As the branches above shout, "More! Who's to say?"

So here's to our antics, let love be a prank,
For joy shared in laughter comes first, then the thanks.
A party of givers with spirits that fly,
Under the tree where our happiness lies!

Threads of Generosity

In a world of threads, let's weave some delight,
With fabric of laughter, oh what a sight!
I stitched up a sweater, it's bright and it's warm,
But on the dog, it's alarmingly a charm.

My neighbor brought cookies, I saw them, I dove,
But found out too late, they were made with "grove."
We laughed and we snacked, though the taste went amiss,

With sprinkles of madness, who could be remiss?

Wrapped gifts and adventures, for each we intend,
Mismatched socks go—Oh, what a trend!
A quilt for a friend, made of patchwork and pride,
And suddenly it's art! Who knew there's a guide?

So here's to the threads that tie us in fun,
Our quirky connections, they shimmer and run.
In this fabric of giving, we revel, we cheer,
Seams made of silly love, the best kind to wear!

Echoes of Compassion

In echoes of laughter, goodwill bounces round,
Our voices unite, like a joyous sound.
With jokes on the shelf, and kindness our game,
We giggle and poke, like it's all the same.

A chicken and a donut sat down for a chat,
"I give you my love, but you're looking quite fat!"
They burst into chuckles, a hilarious scene,
Two foods in the fridge, plotting like a dream.

When friends lend an ear, or throw in some cheer,
A simple kind act can draw us all near.
We dance with the joy, in a comedic way,
And toss out our burdens, come join in the play!

So raise up your voices, let laughter take flight,
In this funny world, may our hearts shine so bright.
With echoes of kindness, together we thrive,
In a symphony of laughter, we love, we survive!

In the Spirit of Sharing

In a spirit of fun, we gather as one,
With quirky ideas, the laughter has spun.
We trade socks and stories, it’s wild and it’s bright,
With mismatched pairs, who gets the last bite?

One friend brings the punch—oh, what a mistake!
It looks like a potion from beyond the lake.
With a wink and a nod, we dare take a sip,
It's magic, we’re told, well just let it rip!

Each gift that we share comes with giggles and glee,
A jar full of giggles, wait, that can’t be me!
Old treasures from times that we’ll never forget,
In a whirl of delight, let our hearts be the debt.

So come join the fun, at this gathering small,
With laughter as currency, we’ll have a ball.
In the spirit of sharing, joy dances and glows,
Among friends and good humor, see how it grows!

Gifts Wrapped in Love

A box with a bow, so bright and bold,
Inside are piped socks, one red, one gold.
I chuckle and giggle, oh what a sight,
Who knew fashion could offer such fright!

A sweater too small, for a lumberjack man,
But hey, it's the thought that counts, that's the plan!
With candy canes stuck in the woolly seams,
It's perfect for holiday crafting dreams.

I wrap up my jokes with a chuckle so wide,
A gift that keeps giving, like a runaway ride.
With giggles and grins, no frowns to be seen,
Each gift brings a smile, like a jester routine!

Oh what fun it is, to prank with a gift,
The laughter it brings makes the spirits lift.
So let the surprises come one after another,
For love, laughter, and gifts, we're all one big brother!

A Treasure of Moments

I found in my attic an old photo frame,
A picture of Aunt Edna, and boy was she tame!
I wrapped it up tight, with a laugh and a snicker,
To see her face when she sees that old sticker!

A jar full of buttons, from coats long gone by,
I gift it with glee, oh my, oh my!
Each button a story, each story a laugh,
It’s a quirky little moment, a treasure to craft!

I packed up some rocks, each with a sweet name,
“Rocky the Rock” was the first one to claim.
With googly eyes glued, they all come alive,
Let’s start a pet rock club, oh my, how they thrive!

Our friendships are treasures, we’ll hold them so dear,
As we share silly gifts, we’re spreading the cheer.
With giggles and stories, our moments will grow,
A treasure of laughter, let the good times flow!

The Light We Share

I gifted my friend a lamp that sways,
It flickers and dances, in clumsy ballet.
With colors that clash, it's a sight to behold,
We laugh till we cry, as our stories unfold!

A pair of bright shades, for a rainy parade,
"Just wear them!" I joked, "And watch the fun fade!"
But they donned them with pride, cheerful and bright,
A rainbow of silliness, what a delight!

I wrapped up a sock, just one, that's the catch,
"Your other foot's lonely, it needs a nice match!"
We giggled with glee in our whacky attire,
Who knew simple gifts could set hearts on fire?

Together we shine, in our goofy array,
The light that we share, brings brightness each day.
With laughter as fuel, we're a whimsical crew,
In the warmth of our moments, each heart feels brand new!

The Beauty of Bestowal

A cactus I wrapped with a joke on a tag,
"Don't hug me too tight, or you'll get a snag!"
I chuckle and hand it, oh what a surprise,
With Grandma's fine china, we can't believe our eyes!

A glitter-filled lava lamp joins in the fun,
Turning our den into a bright disco run.
With sparkles aplenty, and tunes from the past,
We dance with delight, who thought this would last?

An open box filled with socks, tacky and bright,
A colorful pair for every awful night.
As we wear them with pride, what a sight to behold,
The beauty of giving, worth far more than gold!

Each gift brings a grin, a giggle, a cheer,
In sharing a laugh, we've nothing to fear.
With hearts full of joy, we'll pass it around,
In this beautiful dance, we are truly profound!

Footsteps of Charity

When I give away socks, oh what a sight,
Hiding in drawers, they squeal with delight.
A mismatched pair, they always run fast,
But wait, where's my left one? It's gone, what a blast!

I tossed out a book, a tale of sweet lore,
A buddy found it, now he's at the store.
He read it so fast, he flew off in glee,
Said he'd return it - but forgot, oh me!

My old hat went astray, a cap with a flair,
Now some kid's the king, pretending without care.
I miss it a bunch, but he wears it with pride,
Who knew one man's trash could be treasure inside?

So give what you can, let the laughter abound,
Watch others enjoy all the things that you've found.
In the spirit of fun, let the smiles flow wide,
For nothing is better than joy when it's shared side by side.

The Gift of Presence

A knock at the door, the neighbors are here,
They brought potato salad, oh what a cheer!
But who made it? That question's on me,
After one too many, I think it's a mystery!

My friend lent me doughnuts, the sweet, sugary kind,
Two hours later, the box was maligned.
Was it really me? Did I munch them so fast?
I swear I just peeked, but I earned a rep at last!

We laughed and we chatted, a party was made,
Then found out the cat joined the sweet parade!
He nibbled the snacks and drooled on the floor,
Guess who's getting lettuce for snacks evermore?

So bring forth your presence, let laughter take flight,
A moment with friends makes every day bright.
Though the treats may go missing, or end up in fluff,
The joy's in the sharing, it's truly enough!

Unseen Blessings

I found a sweet gift, a set of old keys,
Wondered what lock, might open with ease?
A treasure from youth, or an ancient affair,
Turns out it unlocked my wild son’s hair!

Last month, I donated a shirt with a cheer,
But what came back? A fashion faux pas near!
Now I wear it at home with a grin and some clout,
At least it fits well, when the kids run about!

I once gave a toy that barely would squeak,
A crocodile friend, who was far from unique.
Next day it roared loud with a somewhat weird tune,
Guess I blessed the cat, and it danced ‘round the room!

So when you extend your kindness with flair,
Expect the bizarre, with a grin not a care.
Each unseen blessing will travel your way,
Wrapped in giggles, turning night into day.

Hearts Unwrapped

This morning I baked, with joy I confess,
A batch of fine cookies, I thought, what a mess!
But my friend took a bite and said, 'Oh, my stars!'
Now we barter for snacks like we're driving fancy cars!

A gift of warm hugs, but wait, what's that?
I gave one to my neighbor, who followed the cat!
Now every time I see her, it's an all-out race,
To hug with attention and give her my face!

On my birthday, I tried to provide something nice,
But friends crashed the party, by rolling the dice.
Each one brought a story, a laugh and a cheer,
Leaving me grinning year after year!

So let's keep it rolling, this laughter and glee,
Unwrap all the smiles, so everyone's free.
With hearts open wide, let the mischief abound,
In every small moment, pure joy can be found!

A Symphony of Hearts

A gift of socks with polka dots,
My roommate screams, he likes them lots.
A rubber duck that quacks in tune,
We dance and laugh beneath the moon.

An old guitar that's lost its strings,
I serenade while he pretends to sing.
With every giggle, the joy expands,
Two silly fools with funny plans.

A jar of jam that's sticky sweet,
I spread it thick on his old seat.
He sits and slips and then he slides,
We roll with laughter, oh, what a ride!

Through silly gifts and chuckling cheer,
We share our hearts, we always steer.
A symphony of laughter rings,
In the madness, true joy springs.

The Joyful Exchange

I brought you cookies, lumpy, round,
You gave me socks, their colors abound.
We trade our treasures, what a sight!
Laughter bubbles through the night.

Your gift of crayons, broken, worn,
In my hands, pure art is born.
You look confused, unsure of me,
But trust me mate, I'm crafty free!

I gifted you a cat-shaped hat,
You wore it wrong and on your cat!
The feline squawks, the neighbors frown,
Yet on we go, our smiles drown.

Through silly trades, the moments glow,
In this amusing, wacky show.
Provisioning laughs, oh what a start,
In this merry, light-hearted art.

Kindness in Bloom

A plant I shared, its leaves looked sad,
You said it seemed a little mad.
We danced around it, what a scene,
It perked right up in the playful sheen.

I handed you a squishy toy,
You squeezed it tight with bubbling joy.
It popped on cue, foam flew everywhere,
We spun in craziness, as foam filled the air.

A basket filled with strange delights,
With jars of pickles and spaghetti bites.
We tasted chaos, too much to chew,
With every bite, our friendship grew.

In laughter's bloom, we tend our way,
To silly moments that make us sway.
With every gift, a chuckle's tune,
Our garden grows under the joyful moon.

Mosaics of Generosity

A piece of gum I found today,
You chewed it first, then tossed away.
Yet still we laugh, as sticks we share,
Our sticky tales hang in the air.

Old board games from our younger days,
You flipped the rules in funny ways.
I lost the game, and you did too,
Yet we declared ourselves the winning crew.

A mixtape gifted with songs of old,
Each tune a memory, sometimes bold.
You danced like no one was nearby,
With every note, we dared to fly.

In mischief's hands, we weave our thread,
The laughter's echo, our hearts widespread.
Mosaics formed from gift and jest,
A celebration, we are truly blessed.

Milton Keynes UK
Ingram Content Group UK Ltd.
UKHW020818141124
451205UK00012B/643

9 789916 940396